The Spanish-American War:

America Emerges as a World Power

Edited by
Mary Alice Burke Robinson

The wreck of the USS Maine, *being approached by a Spanish diving crew on the day after the explosion. The loss of the battleship triggered U. S. involvement, and "Remember the* Maine*" became the slogan of Americans in the Spanish-American War. (Pearson, February 1898)*

Discovery Enterprises, Ltd.
Carlisle, Massachusetts

© Discovery Enterprises, Ltd., Carlisle, MA 1998

ISBN 1-57960-015-8 paperback edition
Library of Congress Catalog Card Number 97-78305

10 9 8 7 6 5 4 3 2 1

Printed in the United States of America

Subject Reference Guide:

The Spanish-American War:
America Emerges as a World Power
edited by Mary Alice Burke Robinson

Spanish-American War — U. S. History

Theodore Roosevelt — U. S. History

Cuba-U. S. Relations — U. S. History

Philippines — U. S. History

Photo/Illustration Credits:

Cover art - Cartoon of Teddy Roosevelt, the Hero, 1898,
Harvard College Collection.

All illustrations and photos are credited where they appear in the text.

Dedication:

This book is dedicated to my dear friend,
Mary Alice Stever Wehrle

Table of Contents

Note: A full line of dots in the text indicates the deletion of at least one paragraph.

Background

by
Mary Alice Burke Robinson

The Spanish-American War opened the door to world power for the United States at the turn of the 20th century. In an effort to help free Cuba from Spanish rule, the United States engaged in what Secretary of State John Hay referred to as "a splendid little war; begun with the highest motives, carried on with magnificent intelligence and spirit, favored by that fortune which loves the brave." It was a war in which American journalists played a significant role, rallying citizens into a frenzy of patriotic fervor, often by reporting inaccurate and exaggerated stories, which captured the public's attention.

In addition to the battles in Cuba, American troops fought at Manila Bay, and later in the jungles of the Philippines, at first with the Spain, and then, after the war, with the very Filipino colonists they had freed from Spanish rule.

Only five days after President McKinley declared war on Spain, Navy Admiral George Dewey destroyed the Spanish fleet at Manila Bay. The war efforts in Cuba were almost as swift, with the Spaniards surrendering on July 17th, 1898, less than three months after war had been declared.

President McKinley and his war cabinet. (Harper & Brothers, 1898)

In the 1890s, Cuba, a colony of Spain, was struggling to obtain freedom, with the support of Cuban emigrants to the U. S. On February 10, 1896, to put down the Cuban rebel movement spearheaded by Maximo Gomez, Spanish General Valeriano Weyler arrived in Havana, Cuba. Weyler idolized General William Tecumseh Sherman, famous for his ruthless "scorched earth policy" in the South during the American Civil War. Patterned after Sherman's campaign, Weyler instituted a harsh campaign in Cuba, called "Subjugation or Death."

Weyler, referred to as the "Butcher" in the press, planned a harsh strategy. Spanish troops cut all the trees in a 200-yard wide swath from north to south called the *trocha*. Armored cars ran on a military railroad through this tract in the dense jungles. Every quarter mile were forts with watchtowers, armed with cannon and barbed wire entanglements. He ordered his soldiers to burn crops, kill farm animals, poison wells and destroy buildings.

Cuban peasants were herded into towns or camps guarded by the Spanish troops. If the peasants came peacefully, they were promised housing, food, and work. If they resisted, or if they were found outside the areas of confinement, they were shot. The peasants were housed in abandoned warehouses, with no beds, inadequate sanitary facilities, no medical care, and scarcely any food. It is estimated that 400,000 men, women and children died, which represented one quarter of the population of Cuba in the 1890s.

In retaliation for the establishment of Weyler's concentration camps, Cuban rebels destroyed sugar plantations, and burned buildings. If American plantation owners did not support the rebel cause (Cuba Libre), or refused to pay protection money, their property was destroyed. Laborers who continued to work in the sugar factories were considered traitors, and killed. Many peasants joined rebel leader Maximo Gomez, not because of strong feelings about Cuba Libre, but because no sugar crop meant starvation for themselves and their families. When the Cuban sugar economy collapsed, repercussions were felt in the United States.

In 1896, the Spanish government in Cuba forbade tobacco exports. By stopping the exportation of tobacco to the U. S., Cuban cigar makers in Florida would be forced out of work and would stop donating one dollar a week from their salaries for arms and supplies for the insurgents. In retaliation for stopping the exportation of tobacco, the rebels promptly burned tobacco storage barns and tobacco in the fields. The $100 million a year in trade between the U. S. and Cuba dropped to nearly zero.

A Reporter's Notes

Source: Gilson Willets, *The Triumph of Yankee Doodle*, London, F. Tennyson Neely, Publisher, 1898, pp. 201-204.

The province or country of Vuelta Abajo, is, or rather was, Cuba's principal tobacco center. But today every tobacco plantation in Vuelta Abajo is in ruins, abandoned. The direct cause of this whole-sale destruction was Weyler's tobacco decree. All the farmers, farm hands, dealers, and persons directly or indirectly engaged in raising or dealing in tobacco, had hitherto been sacred to the insurgents; all tobacco property was respected, in direct contrast to sugar plantations. No sooner was Weyler's decree known in Vuelta Abajo than the rebels attacked with fury. Over four hundred thousand bales of tobacco (approximating forty million pounds) were destroyed in 1896 and 1897 in Vuelta Abajo, and the war on the weed continues to the present day....

Whole villages and towns have been destroyed; and eighty percent of the population has perished....

As American economic interests in Cuba grew, so did American interest in the political climate there.

In January 1898, President McKinley sent the USS *Maine* to Cuba, supposedly on a good will mission, but in reality to protect American interests, and, if necessary, to rescue Americans. The *Maine* arrived in Havana Harbor on January 25, 1898.

By this time, many American journalists had been sent to Cuba, and their distorted, sensational stories were inflaming Americans with a feeling that it was an American duty to help the rebels in the cause of Cuba Libre. After the explosion and sinking of the USS *Maine* in Havana Harbor on February 15, 1898, President McKinley was called "Wobbly Willie" because of his reluctance to take a firm stand on the matter, and was burned in effigy. McKinley

7

realized that if he wanted to maintain his party leadership, he must bow to public opinion, and abandon his position of neutrality.

In March, 1898, Congress provided $50 million to increase the size and strength of the American armed forces. On April 20, Congress adopted a resolution to intervene in Cuba. The next day the United States established a blockade of Cuba and severed relations with Spain. On April 24, Spain declared war on the United States. On the 25th, Congress made its declaration of war on Spain retroactive to the 21st, and President McKinley called for volunteers to enlist in the army and navy. A *Washington Post* article in 1898 stated "The taste of war is in the mouth of the people."

The Yellow Journalists

The Spanish-American War had more news correspondents reporting from Cuba than any previous war in American history. Eager reporters fed the public's craving for sensational and violent news and illustrations.

In its Sunday edition, the New York World *ran a comic strip called "Hogan's Alley" which featured a funny little character dressed in yellow. The popular "Yellow Kid" came to symbolize a style of journalism that differed substantially from the traditional news coverage familiar to Americans.*

William Randolph Hearst, of the New York Journal, *and Joseph Pulitzer, of the* New York World, *carried on a battle for supremacy in newspaper circulation. Pulitzer never quite reached the excesses of yellow journalism that Hearst did, although those two newspapers were by far the most anti-Spanish. Much of the war hysteria was created by the* New York Journal *and the* New York World.

Hearst and Pulitzer sent enthusiastic young writers and illustrators to Cuba, who often used unconfirmed reports and headlined lurid tales of atrocities committed against the oppressed Cubans. After the war began, over 200 reporters went to Cuba, working for newspapers from several cities. Hearst and Pulitzer had press boats stationed in the waters between the U. S. and Cuba.

Spanish officials, outraged by the bravado of the correspondents, offered rewards for their capture. General Weyler offered $10,000 for information leading to the capture of Sylvester Scovel, a particularly headstrong reporter.

The Journal's *bold motto was: "While Others Talk, the Journal Acts," and that was certainly evident in events preceding and during the Spanish-American War.*

Where's the War?

Source: James Creelman, *On the Great Highway: The Wanderings and Adventures of a Special Correspondent*, Boston, Lothrop Publishing Company, 1901, pp. 177-178.

Some time before the destruction of the battleship *Maine* in the harbor of Havana, the *New York Journal* sent Frederic Remington, the distinguished artist, to Cuba. He was instructed to remain there until the war began; for 'yellow journalism' was alert and had an eye for the future.

Presently Mr. Remington sent this telegram from Havana:

W. R. HEARST, *New York Journal*, N.Y.:

Everything is quiet. There is no trouble here. There will be no war. I wish to return.

Remington.

This was the reply:

REMINGTON, HAVANA:

Please remain. You furnish the pictures, and I'll furnish the war.

W. R. Hearst.

The proprietor of the *Journal* was as good as his word, and to-day the gilded arms of Spain, torn from the front of the palace in Santiago de Cuba, hang in his office in Printing House Square, a lump of melted silver, taken from the smoking deck of the shattered Spanish flagship, serves as his paper weight, and the bullet-pierced headquarters flag of the Eastern army of Cuba...adorns his wall.

"The **Journal** *Acts"*

Hearst and his journalists performed acts that went far beyond the law. Here is one example:

Source: *Ibid.*, pp. 189-190.

There are times when public emergencies call for the sudden intervention of some power outside of governmental authority. Then journalism acts. Let me give an instance.

When Admiral Camara was preparing to sail with a powerful Spanish fleet to attack Admiral Dewey in Manila Bay, two American monitors armed with ten-inch rifles were on their way across the Pacific to the Philippines. It was a perilous situation, more perilous than the American people were permitted to know. I have seen Admiral Dewey's letters to Consul General Wildman at Hong Kong, begging for news of the movements of the Spanish fleet and confessing that his squadron was too weak to meet it unless the two monitors should arrive in time. The threatened admiral made no secret of his anxiety. The question of victory or defeat or retreat depended on whether the Spanish fleet could be delayed until the powerful monitors had time to reach Manila.

In that critical hour, when the statesmen at Washington were denouncing 'yellow journalism,' I received the following message in the London office of the *New York Journal*:

Dear Mr. Creelman:

I wish you would at once make preparations so that in case the Spanish fleet actually starts for Manila we can buy some big English steamer at the eastern end of the Mediterranean and take her to some part of the Suez Canal where we can then sink her and obstruct the passage of the Spanish warships. This must be done if the American monitors sent from San Francisco have not reached Dewey and he should be placed in a critical position by the approach of Camara's fleet. I understand that if a British vessel were taken into the canal and sunk under the circumstances outlined above, the British Govern-

ment would not allow her to be blown up to clear a passage and it
might take time enough to raise her to put Dewey in a safe position.

Yours very truly,
W. R. Hearst.

THE BIG TYPE WAR OF THE YELLOW KIDS.

*Publishers Joseph Pulitzer and William Randolph Hearst competed with
each other over covering the Spanish-American War. When Hearst stole the
famous cartoon character, "The Yellow Kid" from Pulitzer, the new style
of sensationalist writing that followed was called "yellow journalism."
(Library of Congress)*

Spanish and American Military

The United States army was small, with between 24,000 and 30,000 men, most of whom were stationed in the West. On April 25, 1898, President McKinley issued a call for volunteers to join the armed forces. The response was immediate, and too successful. The army was woefully unprepared to handle the more than 200,000 who answered the president's call. The army lacked everything: equipment, food, training, organization. The only uniforms were woolen. There were no boots, bedding, or mosquito netting.

General Shafter was overwhelmed by the logistics of an amphibious campaign. Tampa, Florida, serving as the point of departure for troops, was too small to accommodate the large numbers of men and horses that swarmed down on the little city which had only one railroad line. It lacked water and proper sanitation. Almost immediately, dysentery and typhus struck.

Several of the cavalry units were forced to leave their horses in Tampa when they finally boarded transports. Transports were privately-owned vessels with civilian captains and crews who could not be relied on to follow orders. Soldiers were aboard the transports for eight days. In addition, the press boats were running in and around the transports, landing their correspondents on the shore ahead of the soldiers.

The troops landed in no particular order, jumping onto a wooden pier which had been damaged by Spanish soldiers the night before. With one hundred rounds of ammunition, bedrolls, and other equipment, many went crashing through gaps in the planking, suffering injuries before they had seen any military action.

The army landed unopposed near Santiago, and by evening six thousand troops had landed, with only two fatalities. The next day, two regiments had landed at Siboney, eight miles east.

U. S. troops en route to Santiago in 1898. (Harper)

Dr. Nicholas Senn was chief surgeon with the army. His letters provide a first-hand account of the problems faced by the men during the Spanish-American War.

Source: Dr. Nicholas Senn, *War Correspondence*, Chicago, American Medical Association Press, 1899, pp. 77,95, 122-123, 237.

It was not the medical department, but the arrogance or stupidity of the commanding general of the invading army that is responsible for the extensive outbreak of yellow fever...

The Cuban invasion was characterized by hasty action, a lack of organization, and inadequate preparation.

The Cuban and Porto Rican invasions have confirmed the experience of the past in showing that the greatest horrors of war are caused by disease and its consequences rather than the implements of destruction.

The accumulation of large armies and the prolonged encampments in localities which lacked a system of sewerage, could not fail in promoting the local spread of infectious disease.

Source: Richard Harding Davis, *The Cuban and Porto Rican Campaigns*, Scribner's, NY, 1898, pp. 279-282.

The personal belongings of the officers had been left behind on the transports, and...they never saw razors and fresh linen again until they purchased them in Santiago. A tooth-brush was the only article...to which all seemed to cling, and each of the men carried one stuck in his hat-band, until they appeared to be a part of the uniform.

....

During the week we were camped below El Poso, whenever it rained during the day both officers and men used to stow their clothes under the dog-tent in a rubber poncho and stand about naked until the sun came out again. I have a photograph of one of the officers of the Rough Riders digging his rain-trench while dressed in a gold chain and locket. General Miles was very much amused and startled when he visited the camp of the volunteers from Washington, D.C., to see several hundred of them standing naked at attention and saluting him as he passed.

Although Spain had between 100,000 and 200,000 soldiers in the army in Cuba, many were very young, and others had been forced into the service. The Spanish fleet was outdated and undermanned. The ships had poorly-trained crews, with so little ammunition that they could not practice target shooting. The Spanish fleet was only about one-third the size of the American navy which had grown under the Assistant Secretary of the Navy, Theodore Roosevelt. Our navy had well trained crews aboard new ships, most of which had been built after 1890.

Women in the War

Clemencia Arango

Richard Harding Davis was aboard a ship in February 1897 when he met a young Cuban woman who had been detained and searched by Spanish officials. The story that Davis wrote for the New York Journal *appeared on page one. It was accompanied by Frederic Remington's illustration of a naked girl being questioned by a group of men. The American public was shocked and outraged. The* New York World *responded with a completely different version of Senorita Arango's experience, but the Davis article was the first, the one that carried the more lurid details, and therefore, carried the most weight.*

Source: *New York Journal*, February 12, 1897.

"DOES OUR FLAG SHIELD WOMEN?"

TAMPA, Fla., Feb. 10—On the boat which carried me from Cuba to Key West were three young girls who had been exiled for giving aid to the insurgents. The brother of one of them, Miss Clemencia Arango, is in command of the Cuban forces in the field near Havana. More than once the sister has joined him there and has seen fighting and carried back dispatches to the Junta in Havana. So for this she and two other young women, who were also suspected, were ordered to leave the island.

I happened to sit next to Miss Arango at table on the steamer. I found that she was not an Amazon, or a Joan of Arc, or a woman of the people, with a machete in one hand and a Cuban flag in the other. She was a well bred, well educated young person who spoke three languages and dresses as you see girls dress on Fifth avenue after church on Sunday.

This is what the Spaniards did to these girls.

After ordering them to leave the island on a certain day, they sent detectives to their houses in the morning of that day and had them undressed and searched to discover if they were carrying letters to the Junta at Key West and Tampa. They then, an hour later, searched them at the Custom House as they were leaving for the steamer. They searched them thoroughly, even to the length of taking off their shoes and stockings, and fifteen minutes later, when the young ladies stood at last on the deck of an American vessel, with the American flag hanging from the stern, the Spanish officers followed them there and demanded that a cabin should be furnished them to which the girls might be taken, and they were then again undressed and searched for the third time....

....

...are we to understand that an American citizen, or a citizen of any country, after he has asked and obtained permission to leave Cuba, and is on board an American vessel, is no more safe there and then than he would be in the insurgent camp?...

No one was particularly interested to hear Senorita Arango state that she had been treated courteously, that she had not been strip-searched, and that the search was carried out in a private room by police matrons. Davis' story made much more exciting reading.

Evangelina Cisneros, Revolutionary Heroine

Six months after the Clemencia Arango story appeared in the American newspapers, another one involving a young Cuban woman swept the country.

Evangelina Cisneros' father was a republican sympathizer who had been found guilty of aiding the insurgents, and sentenced to house arrest at a prison colony in Cuba. His two daughters accompanied him.

In August, 1897, William Randolph Hearst received a telegram from Havana stating that Evangelina Cisneros, the great niece of the first president of the provisional republican government, had been sentenced to twenty years imprisonment. The Spanish government accused her of luring Colonel Barriz, the prison commandant, to her house where a band of Cubans were waiting to kill him, but the plan was foiled by alert Spanish soldiers.

Evangelina maintained that Barriz broke into her home and threatened her when she resisted his advances. Men from neighboring houses heard her screams, and came to her aid, but the Colonel's cries brought soldiers. She was arrested, taken to Havana to the Recojidas prison, where she had lived for over a year.

There had been a lull in exciting stories out of Cuba for a few months. The Cisneros affair was just what the Journal *needed to pick up newspaper circulation, and whip up the war frenzy. Hearst sent Karl Decker, a tall blond Southerner, to Cuba, to rescue "the Cuban martyr." The public loved Hearst's story which contained all the elements of a Victorian novel: beautiful maiden, ugly lecher, dashing savior, daring rescue.*

Later that same year, Cisneros and Decker collaborated on a book, recounting Evangelina's story and rescue.

Source: Evangelina Cisneros, *The Story of Evangelina Cisneros*, New York, Continental Publishing Company, 1897, pp. 78-117.

The account of the rescue was written by Decker, who was accompanied to Cuba by two men. They rented a house directly across an alley from Cisneros' cell.

...it was necessary to throw the ladder diagonally across the right angle separating our roof from the azotea. This was the most ticklish business, as the ladder was frail and thrillingly short.

Finally the ladder was in position and the trip across began. No man engaged in that enterprise will ever forget the twelve-foot walk across that sagging decrepit ladder. At one time it swayed from the wall....

As it was a large piece of the weak cornice on which the ladder was resting, went clattering down into the street, waking the warden, who came hastily to the door.

Don Jose looked out into the quiet street. He stood there for a few minutes....Then, convinced that all was safe, he turned and passed back into Recojidas,....

We crept softly across the roof to the window she had indicated. As we reached it we saw her standing before it. She was dressed in a dark colored gown and not easily seen in the gloom inside. She gave one glad little cry and clasped our hands through the bars, calling upon us to liberate her at once....

Bidding her be quiet, we set to work cutting through the iron bar between her and liberty. We selected the third bar on the left side of the window, and began cutting it near the bottom. Our progress was slow, and wearisome,....It was impossible to use the saw quickly, as the bars were not set firmly in the frame, and rattled and rang like a fire alarm every time the saw passed across the iron.

It is hard to believe that the noise, and the presence of three men outside a prison window, would not cause attention unless the warden and guards had been bribed.

Since the men had not finished cutting the bar that night, they returned to their house, hoping that the weakened bar would not be noticed.

Decker continued.

The next day, Wednesday: I was stiff and sore that day, from the climbing and clambering of the night before....

That night they went back to their work.

...the ladder was quickly raised and thrust across the parapet until it rested upon the cornice of the jail. In a second...the lightest man had crossed and was standing on the roof of the jail, Mallory and I holding the ladder....I quickly followed on the vibrating ladder across the gap....

As we reached the window we saw Evangelina standing just within the window....She reached out her hands to us with many little, glad cries, rippling out in whispered Spanish sentences, terms of endearment and friendship, and calling multiplied benedictions down upon our heads for our efforts to save her....

It was almost impossible to keep her quiet, and it was not until Hernandon sternly bade her cease talking that she became silent....

We went to work quickly....I gripped the bar below where the cut was made and locked the handle of the wrench behind my lag. I then gripped the upper part of the bar with the large wrench and

19

swung all my weight forward upon the handle....I felt the bar yield like a piece of cheese, then snap with a clear, ringing sound that we feared must have been heard at the palace. We dropped at once and lay listening for a few seconds but there was no alarm....

Evangelina was by this time on her knees in front of the opening I had made....

In a moment she saw that she could easily pass through, and she looked up into our faces with a smile much as the devout may wear in sight of Paradise, but seldom is it given any man to see such a gleam upon the face of woman....

By this time the fever of hurry was in all our veins. I quickly grasped Evangelina about the waist and lifted her through the bars. In a moment she was out upon the roof and was bursting into a joyous carol to freedom when I clasped my hand over her mouth, and, picking her up in my arms, carried her quickly across the azotea to where the ladder lay. Here no time was lost in leaving the jail roof....

Without the slightest trace of fear, Evangelina climbed over the parapet and down upon the ladder. I reached far out and steadied her until she was started well upon her trip across. Then as I released her hand she ran quickly across, as though on solid ground,....

Dressed in men's clothes, Evangelina boarded a ship and escaped to the United States, where she was treated as a heroine. She was the guest of honor at a huge reception at Madison Square Garden, a banquet at Delmonico's in New York, and was received by President McKinley in Washington.

Cisneros immediately applied for U. S. citizenship. And, after her moment of glory, she soon dropped out of the public's interest.

The USS *Maine*

At 9:40 p.m., on February 15, 1898, a mysterious explosion blew up the USS Maine *as she lay at anchor in Havana Harbor. Of the 354 officers and men on board, 266 were killed. Hearst's* Journal *story took up the full first page, and the slogan, "Remember the* Maine*! To Hell with Spain!" became a battle cry. Newspaper artists drew pictures of where torpedoes or mines had been placed, in spite of the lack of any evidence. The February 16* Journal *devoted eight full pages to the explosion. Circulation reached a new record.*

Two days later, the Journal *published an early edition carrying this banner: "DESTRUCTION OF THE WARSHIP* MAINE *WAS THE WORK OF AN ENEMY," with a drawing of an artist's conception of the explosion. The newspaper also offered a $50,000 reward for information about the perpetrators. In the same article it set forth rumors as fact, and boldly accused Spain for the explosion.*

Rumors were rampant, including one that Hearst had masterminded a plot to blow up the ship to encourage American support for Cuba. Both the United States and Spain held inquiries. The U. S. concluded that the explosion was caused by a mine but blamed no one. Spain said the explosion was inside the ship. Admiral Hyman G. Rickover, in his 1976 book, How the Battleship Maine Was Destroyed, *concluded that the cause was spontaneous combustion in an unventilated coal bunker. Other ships fueled with coal had blown up the same way.*

The Explosion of the USS Maine

George Bronson Rea was sitting in a cafe in Havana on the evening that the Maine *blew up. It was carnival season and the streets were full of revellers. This is Rea's account:*

Source: George Bronson Rea, "The Night of the Explosion in Havana," *Harper's Weekly*, Vol. 42, #2150, Saturday, March 5, 1898, p. 222.

In company with Mr. and Mrs. Sylvester Scovel, the writer was seated in one of the numerous cafes located near the park. Suddenly the sound of a terrible explosion shook the city; windows were broken and doors were shaken from their bolts. The sky towards the bay was lit up with an intense light, and above it all could be seen innumerable colored lights resembling rockets.

Hastily providing for the safety of his wife, Scovel and I jumped into a coach, and ordered the reluctant driver to drive for his life in the direction of the noise. The populace were evidently frightened, probably believing that the explosion was the forerunner of another riot, and very few essayed to leave their doors and venture into the street. As we approached the docks the excitement increased, and at last, reaching the custom-house gate, we found an excited crowd trying to force its way through, despite the energetic remonstrance and resistance of the guards.

Elbowing and pushing through, we informed the guards that we were two officers from the *Maine*; for by this time we understood something terrible had occurred on board. The gates were quickly opened, and closed immediately. Rushing through the baggage-inspection room and out on the open wharf, our worst fears were realized—the *Maine* was a wreck and burning brightly. Jumping into a boat with the chief of police, colonel Paglieri, we were soon out in the harbor. Our progress was often retarded by huge masses of floating wreckage, and as we approached closer, the rapid-fire and small-arm ammunition began to explode and whiz through the air over our heads. Our boatmen were paralyzed with fear, and wished to turn back. The colonel beat one of them with his cane. I whacked the other with a rope's end, until they concluded to proceed.

The scene as it unfolded itself to our vision was terrible in its significance. Great masses of twisted and bent iron plates and beams were thrown up in confusion amidships; the bow had disappeared; the foremast and smoke-stacks had fallen; and to add to the horror and danger, the mass of wreckage amidships was on fire, and at frequent intervals a loud report, followed by the whistling sound of fragments flying through the air, marked the explosion of a 6-pound shell.

The greatest danger for a time seemed to lie in another magazine explosion; but, despite this circumstance, we could see the boats of the Spanish cruiser and of the City of Washington darting in and out of the wreckage, bravely rescuing some poor fellow crying for help. We pulled close to the wreck, in the hope of being of some assistance. We arrived there fifteen minutes after the crash, the first to reach her from the shore, but in that short time everybody who survived had already been saved. Too much praise cannot be bestowed on the crews and officers of the two steamers mentioned, who were on the spot immediately after the catastrophe, and their vessels did not draw away for more than three-quarters of an hour after, or when it was deemed absolutely necessary to protect themselves from the danger of being struck by fragments of the shells and fixed ammunition which were constantly exploding....

We finally comprehended the full extent of the calamity....The stern old Spanish colonel muttered, 'Ave Maria! how horrible!' and, with another oath, made a pass at the boatmen with his cane, to urge them forward to where we could now discern the forms of Captain Sigsbee and his officers—many of them half-dressed—standing in their boats sadly viewing the remnants of their once-proud cruiser. Here we were hastily informed of what had occurred. At this time it was impossible to estimate the loss of life, and many were supposed to have been saved by swimming to other vessels. We followed Captain Sigsbee to the gang-way of the Washington, and there the chief of police offered his services and expressed his sympathy to the Captain....

...a large deputation of prominent Spanish officials, headed by

Secretary-General Congosto, arrived on board to express their sympathy, and to offer all the aid in their power. Their attentions were kindly received and answered by Captain Sigsbee, and when they left the ship I accompanied them ashore, and I must say that I only heard the most profound expressions of sympathy and sorrow. When Dr. Congosto learned that I was the bearer of the official and private telegrams of the Captain and officers, he sent orders to the cable-office that all telegrams I might present for transmission should be given the right of way, and that all expenses should be paid by the Spanish government. This was indeed a delicate compliment to the noble officers who had been left destitute as a result of the explosion, and deserves at least our appreciation.

Surviving injured sailors were taken to Havana hospitals, where Frances Scovel and other American women helped as volunteer nurses and interpreters. An offer by Spanish officials to bury the dead American sailors was accepted by Captain Sigsbee. They were buried in a military cemetery with full honors.

This was a turning point in American-Spanish relations. In a little over two months, America would be at war with Spain.

In March, 1912, the Maine *was finally raised from the ocean floor, towed out of Havana Harbor, and sunk three miles out at sea.*

The Campaign to Take Santiago

After landing at Daiquiri on June 23, the Americans planned a direct assault on Santiago, but in order to do that, they had to pass Las Guasimas, and take the San Juan Heights. A secondary objective was El Caney, a fortified village three miles to the north of the San Juan Hills.

Las Guasimas, The First Encounter

June 24, 1898

Richard Harding Davis was the most respected correspondent of the Spanish-American War. He was in Cuba before the Americans entered into war with Spain, and his stories that appeared in Harper's Magazine *and the* New York Journal *were avidly read. In June, 1898, Davis was with the Americans when they set off for Santiago. Here follow excerpts from his account of the battle at Las Guasimas:*

Source: Davis, *op. cit.*, pp. 135-171.

Guasimas is not a village, nor even a collection of houses; it is the meeting-place of two trails which join at the apex of a V, three miles from the seaport town of Siboney, and continue merged in a single trail to Santiago....

The men had made a night march the evening before, had been given but three hours troubled sleep on the wet ground, and had then been marched in full equipment up hill and under a cruelly hot sun, right into action....To this handicap was also added the nature of the ground and the fact that our men could not see their opponents....

No flankers were placed for the reason that the dense under-growth and the tangle of vines that stretched from the branches of the trees to the bushes below make it a physical impossibility for man or beast to move forward except along the beaten path....

If each trooper had not kept in touch with the man on either hand he would have been lost in the thicket....

In a few minutes they all broke through into a little open place in front of a dark curtain of vines, and the men fell on one knee and began returning the fire that came from it....

The enemy were hidden in the shade of the jungle, while they (Americans) had to fight in the open for every thicket they gained, crawling through grass which was as hot as a steam bath, and with their flesh and clothing torn by thorns and the sword-like blade of the Spanish "bayonet." The glare of the sun was full in their eyes and as fierce as a limelight....

Wounded Spanish prisoners at Brigade hospital. (War Dept.)

General Shafter sent General George Lawton with 6900 men to attack El Caney at dawn on July 1. After taking El Caney the soldiers would start toward the San Juan hills to help support 5200 infantrymen and 2700 troopers of the 9th Regular Cavalry (a black unit) in their taking of the village of San Juan, Kettle Hill and the Heights. General Lawton soon realized that more than two hours were needed to take El Caney. The delay here caused the whole battle plan to disintegrate.

"Wasn't It A Splendid Fight?"

The Battle at El Caney

James Creelman, one of the "Yellow Journalists," was with American forces when they made their assault on the Spanish fort at El Caney on July 1, 1898. He himself was wounded that day. This is Creelman's account of how he came into possession of a Spanish flag which he was determined to present to his boss, William Randolph Hearst, who personally took down Creelman's story as Creelman lay wounded near the battlefield.

Source: Creelman, *op, cit.*, pp. 195-212.

At last I reached the top of a little hill, so close to the gray fort, with its red and yellow flag streaming above its walls, that I could see the Spanish faces under the row of straw hats in the outlying trench on the slope, and the shining barrels of the Mauser rifles projecting over the earthworks. Capron's battery, a mile and a half away, was hurling shells at the fort;....

The only sign of life about the fort itself was a black hen that ran out of an open door at the side and fluttered excitely along the foot of the wall....

Now the Twelfth Infantry began to press its brown ranks of cracking riflery into the sheltered gullies in front of the fort, and Company C, throwing itself face down on the hill where I sat, sent a steady fire into the Spanish trench. The Spaniards returned the volleys, but one by one we could see them fall behind the breastworks, here and there a leg or arm sticking up. The living men in the trench cowered down. But still the bullets came ting-ing, and the hilltop was strewn with our dead and dying....

Nothing moved at the fort but the black hen. As volley after volley swept the hill, she dashed to and fro, growing angrier every moment. Her feathers stood on end and she pecked savagely at the air. A more indignant fowl never trod the earth. She flapped her wings and hopped into fighting attitudes as the bullets spattered around her. I could hear the soldiers laughing as the hen ran from side to side, believing that the whole battle was directed against herself. Poor creature! She escaped ten thousand bullets only to have her neck wrung by a hungry soldier that night....

Leaving the hill on which I had watched the fight for hours,—with occasional efforts to bandage the wounded or drag the dead off the firing line,—I went to the next ridge, where Chaffee and his two regiments were facing the main intrenchments of the village. By this time the infantry volleying was terrific. Dead and dying men and officers could be seen everywhere. The Spaniards were selling their sovereignty dearly.

The 7th Infantry during the assault on El Caney, July 1, 1898 (Harper)

After some time, the officers decided to charge the fort. Creelman went along, armed only with a revolver.

It was only three hundred feet to the top of the hill, and yet the slope looked a mile long....

There was the Spanish flag, a glorious prize for my newspaper....

In less time than it takes to write it, the trench was crossed and the open door at the end of the fort was reached. The scene inside was too horrible for description. Our fire had killed most of the garrison, and the dead and wounded lay on the floor in every conceivable attitude. A wail of terror went up from helpless men writhing in their own blood. Just inside the door stood a young Spanish officer, surrounded by his men. His face was bloodless, and his lips were drawn away from his teeth in a ghastly way. Beside him was a soldier holding a ramrod, to which was fastened a white handkerchief,–a mute appeal for life....

The officer threw his hands up....Did he understand that if his men fired another shot his safety could not be assured? Yes, yes, yes! and every Spaniard dropped his weapon....

I looked above the roofless walls for the flag. It was gone. A lump came in my throat. The prize had disappeared....

'A shell carried the flag away,' said the Spanish officer. 'It is lying outside.'

Dashing through the door and running around to the side facing El Caney, I saw the red and yellow flag lying in the dust, a fragment of the staff still attached to it. I picked it up and wagged it at the intrenched village. A wiser man would have refrained from that challenge; but I was not wise that day. Instantly the Spanish intrenchments on the village slopes replied with volleys, and I ran,...to the other side of the fort....

Although bullets were beating around the door of the fort, Captain Haskell...agreed to enter and assure the prisoners of their safety. We went in and, while we stood talking to the Spanish officer, I felt a stinging pain in the upper part of the left arm, as though a blow had been struck with a shut fist. The sensation was no more and no less than that which might have come from a rough punch by some too hilarious friend. It whirled me half around but did not knock me down. The next moment there was a numbness in the arm, a darting pain in the hand and a sharp sensation in the back—the arm hung loose as though it did not belong to me. A Mauser bullet, entering one of the loopholes, had smashed the arm and torn a hole in my back....

It is not necessary to describe how I staggered to a hammock in a compartment of the fort and lay there, hearing my own blood drip, how Major John Logan and five of his gallant men passed me out of the fort through a hole made by our artillery, and how I was carried down the hill and laid on the roadside among the wounded, with the captured Spanish colors thrown over me.

Our troops were still fighting their way into the village, and we could hear the savage rip-rip-ripping of the rifles in the distance and hear the calling of the bugles....

Then an American flag was carried past us on its way to the fort and brave old Colonel Haskell, with bullet holes in his neck and leg, lifted himself painfully on one elbow to greet it. A wounded negro soldier, lying flat on his back, raised his bloody hand to his head in salute. Bullets sang above the heads of the surgeons as they bent over the victims....

Some one knelt in the grass beside me and put his hand on my fevered head. Opening my eyes, I saw Mr. Hearst, the proprietor of the *New York Journal*, a straw hat with a bright ribbon on his head, a revolver at his belt, and a pencil and note-book in his hand. The man who had provoked the war had come to see the result with his own eyes and, finding one of his correspondents prostrate, was doing the work himself. Slowly he took down my story of the fight. Again and again the tinging of the Mauser bullets interrupted. But he seemed unmoved. That battle had to be reported some-how....

'I'm sorry you're hurt, but'—and his face was radiant with enthusiasm—'wasn't it a splendid fight? We must beat every paper in the world.'

After doing what he could to make me comfortable, Mr. Hearst mounted his horse and dashed away for the seacoast, where a fast steamer was waiting to carry him across the sea to a cable station.

The Taking of San Juan

July 1, 1898

The only practical route from El Poso to the San Juan Heights was a narrow trail, bordered on both sides by dense jungle vegetation, then opening up into a meadow at the base of the Heights. There the Americans were in full view, unprotected from enemy fire. From the ford of the Aguadores River, and of the San Juan River, the Americans were within range of the Spanish guns.

Davis' admiration for the men who fought was evident as was his critical attitude toward many of the officers, especially General Shafter. Davis thought the whole campaign was badly managed and caused unnecessary suffering and fatalities.

Source: Davis, *op. cit.*, pp. 193-194, 211-213.

The place hardly needs a map to explain it. The trails were like a pitchfork, with its prongs touching the hills of San Juan. The long handle of the pitchfork was the trail over which we had just come, the joining of the handle and the prongs were El Poso. El Caney lay half way along the right prong, the left one was the trail down which, in the morning the troops were to be hurled upon San Juan. It was as yet an utterly undiscovered country....

Before the moon rose again, every sixth man who had slept in the mist that night was either killed or wounded....

Davis told of the devastating effect of an observation balloon, the crush of men and the merciless fire from the Spanish.

The observation balloon hastened the end. It came blundering down the trail, and stopped the advance of the First and Tenth Cavalry, and was sent up directly over the heads of our men to observe what should have been observed a week before by scouts and reconnoitering parties...a balloon on the advance line, and only fifty feet above the tops of the trees, was merely an invitation to the enemy to kill everything beneath it. And the enemy responded to the invitation.

31

A Spaniard might question if he could hit a man, or a number of men, hidden in the bushes, but had no doubt at all as to his ability to hit a mammoth glistening ball only six hundred yards distant, and so all the trenches fired at it at once, and the men of the First and Tenth, packed together directly behind it, received the full force of the bullets. The men lying directly below it received the shrapnel which was timed to hit it, and which at last, fortunately, did hit it. This was endured for an hour, an hour of such hell of fire and heat, that the heat in itself, had there been no bullets, would have been remembered for its cruelty. Men gasped on their backs, like fish in the bottom of a boat, their heads burning inside and out, their limbs too heavy to move. They had been rushed here and rushed there wet with sweat and wet with fording the streams, under a sun that would have made moving a fan an effort, and they lay prostrate, gasping at the hot air, with faces aflame, and their tongues sticking out, and their eyes rolling.

A young private also recorded his experiences that day:

Source: Charles Johnson Post, *The Little War of Private Post*, Little, Brown, New York, 1960, pp. 169-179, .

Three regiments were now in the trail, and it was jammed. Companies were mixed up. Officers and sergeants were shouting to keep their units intact....It was no march, it was a weaving, shuffling mass of men, crouching, halting, crouching again, and always pressing forward over the rough path of the trail....

The trail was so thick with men that I found myself with M Company and with a couple of Ninth Infantrymen alongside...

And we all jostled along together—three regiments of us in that one cowpath!...

Because Lieutenant Colonel Derby's balloon had told the Spaniards we were in that cowpath, they turned all they had upon it and its approach. Over four hundred men were killed or wounded in that trail and at that ford, in an area that was, perhaps, a city block in length—some eight hundred feet—in a path not as wide as a city sidewalk.

Confusion reigned as men got separated from their units, and the crush forced the soldiers up front to ford the river or spread out along its banks, under punishing fire of the enemy. The ford across the Aguadores River was later called "Hell's Crossing" and the trail beyond it became known as "Bloody Angle."

Beyond, we could hear the louder reports of our own men who had already crossed the ford and were sheltered by a little bank back from the farther shore. But these were only glimpses; where we were was a crowded mob of men pressing steadily forward. My foot slipped, and I looked down. The trail underfoot was slippery with mud. It was a mud made by the blood of the dead and wounded, for there had been no showers that day. The trail on either side was lined with the feet of fallen men and the sprawled arms of those who could not quite make it.

This was Bloody Ford....

Theodore Roosevelt and the Rough Riders

As soon as the war began, Theodore Roosevelt resigned as Under-Secretary of the Navy, and with his friend, Dr. Leonard Wood, organized the First U. S. Volunteer Cavalry. Unlike Roosevelt, Wood had seen action before. He had received the Medal of Honor for taking part in the capture of Geronimo, the Apache chief.

The cavalry unit that the two men organized was made up of 1000 men from every walk of life and every geographical region. The mayor of Prescott, Arizona, the marshall of Dodge City, Kansas, college athletes, gamblers, cowboys, Indians, blacks, Texas Rangers, Jews, Christian clergy,—all enthusiastically answered the call. They mostly came from Arizona, New Mexico, Oklahoma, and Indian Territory, but there were men from every state, as well as from Australia and Canada.

Buffalo Bill Cody had a popular travelling wild west show. One of the acts was called, "Rough Riders of the World." Because this new volunteer unit caught the popular imagination, its members came to be called Rough Riders, Teddy's Terrors, and, later, Wood's Weary Walkers. (Like the black Tenth Cavalry, they became a dismounted cavalry unit when most of the horses were left in Tampa).

The Rough Riders were a colorful, romantic group, and very devoted to their leaders, Wood and Roosevelt. When Wood replaced a wounded officer in another unit, Roosevelt was given command. His men followed him unquestioningly, even though some critics now say that his leadership was foolhardy, leading to unnecessary loss of life. Rough Riders, however, took great pride in their unit and in serving under Roosevelt.

Roosevelt with his men, 1898 (Library of Congress)

Devoted to his troops...

Colonel Roosevelt was always out in front, leading charges, encouraging his men, and inspiring them with his defiance of death. Yet he won their devotion in another way, too. He sincerely cared for them. One of his men, Trooper Burkholder, of Phoenix, Arizona, told this little story about Colonel Roosevelt. It indicates the mutual admiration and affection between the Rough Riders and their officer.

Source: James Rankin Young, *Thrilling Stories of the War by Returned Heroes*, W. A. Hixenbaugh & Co., Omaha, 1898, pp. 195-196.

It happened at La Quasina. The men were tired with the hard march and hunger was gnawing at every stomach.

...Well, things hadn't improved a bit...when the Colonel began to move about...speaking encouragingly to each group....Shortly afterward we saw the Colonel, his cook, and two of the troopers of Company I strike out along the narrow road toward the town, and we wondered what was up.

It was probably an hour or so after this, and during a little resting spell in our work of clearing ground and making things a little camp-like, that the savory and almost forgotten odor of beef stew began to sweep through the clearing. Men who were working stopped short and began to sniff, and those who had stopped work for a breathing spell forgot to breathe for a second. Soon they joined in the sniffing, and I'll wager every one of us was sniffing as hard as he knew how. Oh, but didn't that smell fine! We weren't sure that it was for us, but we had a smell of it anyway. Quickly drooping spirits revived, and as the fumes of the boiling stew became stronger the humor of the men improved. We all jumped to our work with a will, and picks, shovels and axes were plied in race-horse fashion, while the men would stop now and then to raise their heads and draw a long breath and exclaim: Wow! but that smells good.'

We were finally summoned to feed, and then you can imagine our surprise. There was a big boiler and beside it a crowd of mess tent-men dishing out real beef stew! We could hardly believe our eyes, and I had to taste mine first to make sure it wasn't a dream. You should have seen the expressions on the faces of the men as they gulped down that stew, and we all laughed when one New York man yelled out: 'And it's got real onions in it, too!'

After we had loaded up we began to wonder where it all came from and then the two Troop I men told how the colonel had purchased the potatoes and onions while his own cook secured the meat from Siboney.

You probably won't believe it, but the bushel of potatoes cost Colonel Roosevelt almost $60, and he had to pay thirty odd good American dollars to get the onions, but then he knew what his men wanted, and it was always his men first with him. There was a rush to his tent when we learned this, and if you ever heard the cheering I'm sure you wouldn't wonder why the Rough Riders all love their colonel.

Kettle Hill

American units moved into positions to attack the San Juan Heights. Roosevelt and the Rough Riders headed toward Kettle Hill, so named for the huge kettles that had been used in sugar making. They lay near a deserted blue farmhouse at the top of the hill.

Source: Davis, *op. cit.*, pp. 196-199, 214-223.

The Rough Riders been ordered to halt in the yard of the farm-house, and the artillery horses were drawn up in it, under the lee of the hill. The First and Tenth dismounted Cavalry were encamped a hundred yards from the battery along the ridge. Later I took pains to find out by whose order these troops were placed within such close proximity to a battery, and was informed, by the general in command of the division, that his men had been put in that exact spot by the order of the Commanding General. They might as sensibly have been ordered to paint the rings in a target while a company was firing at the bull's eye. For the first twenty shots the enemy made no reply, when they did it was impossible, owing to their using smokeless powder, to locate their guns. The third shell fell in among the Cubans in the block-house and among the Rough Riders and the men of the First and Tenth Cavalry, killing some and wounding many. These casualties were utterly unnecessary and were due to the stupidity of whoever placed the men within fifty yards of guns in action....Military experts say that the sixty guns left behind in Tampa would have been few enough for the work they had to do. It was like going to a fire with a hook and ladder company and leaving the hose and the steam-engines in the engine-house.

Spanish guns and guerrilla sharpshooters had the Americans pinned down. It became obvious that the Americans were suffering as many casualties as they would if they had attacked. Finally the order was given to advance.

To charge earthworks held by men with modern rifles, and using modern artillery, until after the earthworks have been shaken with artillery, and to attack them in advance and not in the flanks, are

37

both impossible military propositions. But this campaign had not been conducted according to military rules, and a series of military blunders had brought seven thousand American soldiers into a chute of death, from which there was no escape except by taking the enemy who held it by the throat, and driving him out and beating him down....

The rocks on either side were spattered with blood and the rank grass was matted with it....Except for the clatter of the land-crabs, those hideous orchid-colored monsters that haunt the places of the dead, and the whistling of the bullets in the trees, the place was as silent as a grave. For the wounded lying along its length were as still as the dead beside them....

The fight had now lasted an hour, and the line had reached a more open country, with a slight incline upward toward a wood, on the edge of which was a ruined house....The advance upon the ruined building was made in stubborn, short rushes, sometimes in silence, and sometimes firing as we ran....

Roosevelt, who had picked up a carbine and was firing occasionally to give the direction to the others, determined upon a charge. Wood, at the other end of the line, decided at the same time upon the same manoeuvre. It was called "Wood's bluff" afterward, for he had nothing to back it with; while to the enemy it looked as though his whole force was but the skirmish-line in advance of a regiment.

Finally, after heavy fighting, the Spaniards were driven back.

Davis continued:

According to the statement of the enemy, who had every reason not to exaggerate the size of his own force, 4,000 Spaniards were engaged in this action. The Rough Riders numbered 534, of whom 8 were killed and 34 wounded, and General Young's force numbered 464, of which there were 8 killed and 18 wounded. The American troops accordingly attacked a force over four times their own number intrenched behind rifle-pits and bushes in a mountain-pass.

Roosevelt's 'Crowded Hour'

The Taking of Kettle Hill

Roosevelt describes the scene at Kettle Hill.

Source: Theodore Roosevelt, "The Cavalry at Santiago," *Scribner's Magazine*, Vol. 25, #4, April, 1899, pp. 424-430.

Our orders had been of the vaguest kind, being simply to march to the right and connect with Lawton—with whom, of course, there was no chance of our connecting....

The fight was now on in good earnest, and the Spaniards on the hills were engaged in heavy volley firing. The Mauser bullets drove in sheets through the trees and the tall jungle grass, making a peculiar whirring or rustling sound; some of the bullets seemed to pop in the air, so that we thought they were explosive; and indeed, many of those which were coated with brass did explode, in the sense that the brass coat was ripped off, making a thin plate of hard metal with jagged edge, which inflicted a ghastly wound....

While we were lying in reserve we were suffering nearly as much as afterward when we charged. I think that the bulk of the Spanish fire was practically unaimed...but they swept the whole field of battle up to the edge of the river, and man after man in our ranks fell dead or wounded, although I had the troopers scattered out far apart, taking advantage of every scrap of cover.

General Sumner had obtained authority to advance from Lieutenant Miley, who was representing General Shafter at the front and was in the thick of the fire....

The instant I received the order I sprang on my horse, and then my 'crowded hour' began....

...the two rearmost lines of the regiment began to crowd together; so I rode through them both, the better to move on the one in front.

This happened with every line in succession, until I found myself at the head of the regiment.

The Ninth Regiment was immediately in front of me, and the First on my left, and these went up Kettle Hill with my regiment.... General Sumner in person gave the Tenth the order to charge the hills; and it went forward at a rapid gait. The three regiments went forward more or less intermingled, advancing steadily and keeping up a heavy fire.

By this time we were all in the spirit of the thing and greatly excited by the charge, the men cheering and running forward between shots....

Richard Harding Davis observed the charge in a less romantic light.

Source: Davis, *op. cit.*, pp. 217-219.

I have seen many illustrations and pictures of this charge on the San Juan hills, but none of them seem to show it just as I remember it. In the picture-papers the men are running uphill swiftly and gallantly, in regular formation, rank after rank, with flags flying, their eyes aflame, and their hair streaming, their bayonets fixed, in long, brilliant lines, an invincible, overpowering weight of numbers.

Instead of which I think the thing which impressed one the most, when our men started from cover, was that they were so few. It seemed as if someone had made an awful and terrible mistake. One's instinct was to call to them to come back. You felt that someone had blundered and that these few men were blindly following out some madman's order. It was not heroic, it seemed merely terribly pathetic. The pity of it, the folly of such a sacrifice was what held you.

They had no glittering bayonets, they were not massed in regular array. There were a few men in advance, bunched together, and creeping up a steep, sunny hill, the tops of which roared and flashed with flame. The men held their guns pressed across their breasts and stepped heavily as they climbed. Behind these first few, spreading out like a fan, were single lines of men, slipping and scrambling in the smooth grass, moving forward with difficulty, as though they were wading waist high through water, moving slowly, carefully, with strenuous effort. It was much more wonderful than any swinging charge could have been.

Roosevelt told of reaching the top of Kettle Hill.

Source: Roosevelt, *op. cit.*, p. 432.

Wheeling around, I then again galloped toward the hill, passing the shouting, cheering, firing men....Almost immediately afterward the hill was covered by the troops, both Rough Riders and the colored troopers of the Ninth, and some men of the First. There was the usual confusion, and afterward there was much discussion as to exactly who had been on the hill first. The first guidons planted there were those of the three New Mexican troops, G, E, and F, of my regiment, under their Captains, LLewellen, Luna, and Muller, but on the extreme right of the hill, at the opposite end from where we struck it, Captains Taylor and McBlain and their men of the Ninth were first up. Each of the five captains was firm in the belief that his troop was first up.

The official report of the Secretary of War stated positively that two troops of the Ninth gained the crest first.

After the Rough Riders and black soldiers took Kettle Hill, they turned their guns toward San Juan Hill, where the Spanish guns continued to inflict severe punishment on the American infantry units. Soon after the unmounted cavalry came to the aid of the infantrymen, Gatling guns were successfully placed on the south side of Kettle Hill. These machine guns turned the tide in favor of the Americans.

Taking San Juan

A brief account of the battle at San Juan, as described by Roosevelt.

Source: Roosevelt, *op. cit.*, pp. 434-435.

There was very great confusion at this time, the different regiments being completely intermingled—white regulars, colored regulars, and Rough Riders....We were still under a heavy fire, and I got together a mixed lot of men and pushed on from the trenches and ranch houses which we had just taken, driving the Spaniards through a line of palm trees and over the crest of a chain of hills. When we reached these crests we found ourselves overlooking Santiago.

I now had under me all the fragments of the six cavalry regiments which were at the extreme front....

The youngest Rough Rider from Arizona, Arthur L. Tuttle, was interviewed in 1963 by Charles Herner, an historian from Tucson, Arizona. This is Tuttle's recollection of the death of the colorful Bucky O'Neill, who flaunted death by strolling among his men while bullets flew all around him.

Source: Arthur L. Tuttle, Oral interview recorded by Charles Herner, 1963.

Then we moved forward. We crossed a running stream that run down this valley. We were in plain view of the Spaniards. We were ordered to lie down. It was then that several of our men were hit. Our captain Bucky O'Neill was killed but he was quoted as saying there wasn't ever the Spanish bullet has been cast that could kill him. Whether he did or not, or whether he actually believed it. He was talking to another officer. I couldn't hear what they were saying. I was about fifteen feet from him, I was looking right square at him when I heard the bullet. You could hear the bullet hitting. It was a sort of a spat, you know. The bullet went into his open mouth and severed his backbone at the base of his skull. He just collapsed like that, you know. He was dead before he ever hit the ground.

William Payne was a black sergeant of Troop E, Tenth Cavalry (dis-mounted), when he took part in the Spanish-American War. He kept a record of his experiences, and mentioned the support that the well-disciplined black troops gave to the Rough Riders.

Source: Herschel V. Cashin, et al, *Under Fire with the Tenth U. S. Cavalry*, University Press of Colorado, 1993, p. 222.

We remained at San Juan River about three hours. Then came the advance for the bloody charge up San Juan Hill, which we did in good order. This was the second time we came to the rescue of the Rough Riders.

The Tenth Cavalry at Las Guasimas, June 24, 1898. (Harper)

Another black soldier, Sergeant Presly Holliday, of Troop B, Tenth Cavalry, recorded his battle experiences.

Source: *Ibid.*, p. 238.

...we ascended San Juan Hill with Troop F. There I again fell in with Captain Watson and we assembled a little squad of our men and moved up the hill, he ordering us into position to begin firing, but as the plateau just in front of us was full of our own men we did not fire. The Spaniards were just in front retreating. Our men pushed on in pursuit, highly elated at their victory. Captain Jones held F under admirable control, as in many instances discipline was thrown to the winds; indeed, in some cases there was no semblance of organization and the men that pursued the fleeing enemy till he was safe behind intrenchments were little else than howling mobs. Excitement ran high. I saw men so excited that they pointed their guns into the air and fired. Some wanted to fire right through our men in front into the enemy. Captain Jones drew his saber and had to almost take hold of some of the men to prevent them firing; some fired anyhow. About a hundred yards to my right a platoon of Rough Riders knelt in line and asked if there was no officer to give the commands of firing, as they saw some of the enemy far ahead. I ran to them, yelling at the top of my voice, and warned them those were our men just in front of them. They did not fire.

After heavy fighting, the Spaniards withdrew to Santiago.

Source: Roosevelt, *op.cit.*, pp. 439-440.

In the attack on the San Juan hills our forces numbered about 6,600. There were about 4,500 Spaniards against us. Our total loss in killed and wounded was 1,071. Of the cavalry division there were, all told, some 2,300 officers and men, of whom 375 were killed and wounded. In the division over a fourth of the officers were killed or wounded their loss being relatively half as great again as that of the enlisted men—which was as it should be.

The fighting continued throughout the day and continued intermittently all night. The troops began making trenches and to prepare for a siege of Santiago.

On July 3, a truce gave both sides time for badly needed rest.

Source: Roosevelt, "In the Trenches," *Scribner's Magazine*, Vol. 25, #5, May, 1899, pp. 581-585.

After the cessation of the three day's fighting we began to get our rations regularly and had plenty of hardtack and salt pork and usually about half the ordinary amount of sugar and coffee. It was not a very good ration for the tropics, however, and was of very little use indeed to the sick and half sick.

Shortly after midday on the tenth fighting began again, but it soon became evident that the Spaniards did not have much heart in it.

On the seventeenth the city formally surrendered and our regiment, like the rest of the army, was drawn up on the trenches. When the American flag was hoisted the trumpets blared and the men cheered, and we knew that the fighting part of our work was over.

As soon as the surrender was assured the refugees came streaming back in an endless squalid procession down the Caney road to Santiago. My troopers, for all their roughness and their ferocity in fight, were rather tenderhearted than otherwise, and they helped the poor creatures, especially the women and children, in every way, giving them food and even carrying the children and the burdens borne by the women....Finally the doctor warned us that we must not touch the bundles of the refugees for fear of infection, as disease had broken out and was rife among them. Accordingly I had to put a stop to these acts of kindness on the part of my men; against which action Happy Jack respectfully but strongly protested upon the unexpected ground that 'The Almighty would never let a man catch a disease while he was doing a good action.' I did not venture to take so advanced a theological stand.

The Rough Riders disbanded after the Spanish-American War. The regiment presented their colonel with Frederic Remington's bronze sculpture, "The Bronco Buster." This is the telegram he sent to Remington a few days later.

Source: Douglas Allen, *Frederic Remington and the Spanish-American War*, New York, Crown Publishers, 1971, p. 135.

9/19 1898

My dear Remington:

I think your letter pleased the Rough Riders who saw it, as much as their actions pleased you. It was the most appropriate gift the Regiment could possibly have given me, and the one I would have valued most. I have long looked hungrily at that bronze, but to have it come to me in this precise way seemed almost too good.

Faithfully yours, Theodore Roosevelt

Spanish Admiral Cervera and the Battle of Santiago Harbor

July 3, 1898

In April, 1898, Rear Admiral William T. Sampson, commander of the Atlantic fleet, sent Commodore Winfield Scott Schley with a group of ships called "The Flying Squadron," to blockade Cuba. Sampson had most of his other ships looking for the Spanish navy with orders to search and destroy. The Spanish navy posed a threat to American ships, American ports and to troops landing in Cuba.

Spanish Admiral Pascual Cervera had inadequate supplies of fuel and food. His ships and guns needed repair. The Minister of Marine in Madrid ordered him to leave Santiago, and to face the American ships.

The commander of one of the Spanish ships was taken prisoner after the battle and put on board the converted yacht, the Vixen. *Using the chief engineer as an interpreter, Commander Centrores gave this account:*

Source: Young, *op. cit.*, pp. 134-136.

Knowing the force he would have to encounter, he (Cervera) felt convinced that obedience to these orders would spell 'suicide' to the imprisoned fleet that faced it, and he hesitated about taking the risk.

Then came another despatch, a peremptory one, that left no choice but to obey. It said—'No matter what the consequences are, go to sea at once and fight the enemy.'...

'So I went out,' the Admiral said. 'My plan was to attack your *Brooklyn*, sink or disable her if possible, then run to Havana, raise the blockade there and seek refuge in the harbor, but I failed in my purpose, as you know, lost all I had, my fleet and everything. My country's misfortune and my own are very great.'...

Cervera then spoke of Captain Wainwright of the *Gloucester*, and his brave, big-hearted executive officer, Lieutenant H. Mc. L. P. Huse.

Cervera thanked them both from the bottom of his heart for the manner in which they had stood by the fire-imperilled *Maria Teresa*, whose heated guns made a fearful danger zone and whose magazine threatened to dash the life from every one near by.

Seeing the danger, Cervera begged Lieutenant Huse to shove off from the flaming wreck. 'That gallant and noble officer,' said Cervera, 'replied and said: "No, Admiral, not until I have rescued all your wounded!"'

'I jumped overboard,' said the Admiral, speaking of his own adventures, 'and my son followed me. I could make no headway and would have been drowned had not he helped and borne me up with his younger and stronger arms. While we were struggling in the water the Cubans on shore fired at us but the Americans drove them away and would not allow them to molest us again. Then I was taken on board the *Gloucester* and then to the Admiral.

Of Captain Robley D. Evans, of the *Iowa*, the Admiral spoke in glowing terms. On board that vessel he had been received more as a conqueror than a captive, had been allowed to retain his sword, and had seen the marine guard of the ship stationed to receive him as though he was a visiting admiral instead of a half-drowned and sadly beaten hostage of war.

Eulate, captain of the *Vizcaya*, also spoke in high terms of captain Evans, and appreciated the courtesy of "Fighting Bob" in allowing him to retain his sword, and also for the way in which he allowed the *Vizcaya's* dead to be buried. After the Spanish flag had been wrapped around the bodies, the padre of the *Vizcaya* committed them to the deep, the *Iowa's* guard of marines firing three volleys over the dead.

On July 3, 1898, the Spanish fleet was destroyed. All their ships were lost and half their sailors killed or wounded. One thousand eight-hundred Spanish sailors were captured, pulled out of the water by crews on naval vessels or by some of the press boats. One American sailor died during the battle.

"Remember the Maine*" was shouted by American sailors after the battle. Captain Sigsbee, the former captain of the USS* Maine, *commanded one of the American ships.*

Smoked Yankees

In 1866, Congress authorized the creation of several black regiments. They served mostly in the West, fighting in the Indian Wars. They were called Buffalo Soldiers by the Indians who thought their hair looked like buffalo fur. This was a term of honor. To the western tribes, the buffalo is a sacred animal. The black soldiers were dependable, loyal, and brave, and well disciplined. They had the lowest desertion rates in the army.

Four black regiments received orders to go to Cuba. The Spaniards called them "Smoked Yankees." These black soldiers were feared because of their fierceness and bravery. They saw action at Las Guasimas, Kettle Hill, San Juan Hill, El Caney, and in the Philippines.

When their own officers had been killed, black soldiers followed Teddy Roosevelt during the battles of Kettle Hill and San Juan, and probably made the difference between defeat and victory that day. That fact was played down—or even suppressed in favor of the colorful Rough Riders—as was the fact that they planted the flag at Kettle Hill.

Black regiments had white officers. For most white men, to be assigned to command a black unit was an embarrassment. John Pershing, later to become a hero of World War I, was an exception. Because he admired and respected his men, he was given the nickname, "Nigger Jack," by some of his peers. Later, when he commanded the American Expeditionary Forces, the newspapers changed "Nigger Jack" to the less offensive "Black Jack."

There were many black newspapers in the United States. Most expressed indignation that black officers were not allowed to command soldiers. They kept up a campaign urging black men not to volunteer to go to war unless they could be commanded by black officers.

The Richmond Planet, on May 28, 1898, published a strong article entitled, "Should Negroes Enlist?"

Source: George P. Marks, editor, *The Black Press Views American Imperialism (1898-1900)*, New York, Arno Press and *The New York Times*, 1971, pp. 36-37.

There is nothing in the Constitution of the United States which requires us to engage in a war of conquest....

The nation's honor is not at stake, neither is the government in peril. Then, under what obligations are we to be hanging around the front door of the war department gazing at the sign 'Negroes not wanted! Negro officers not thought about!'

Spain, so far as her crimes are concerned, is no more guilty than the United States of America when gauged by the stern rule of comparison.

The two hundred and fifty years of slavery, leaving in its wake broken-hearted mothers, quivering fathers, sobbing children, and streams of blood drawn by the lash, tell a story almost too horrible for reference.

Peace did not bring a cessation of the evil, and murders of the most outrageous kind have been tolerated, and robbery of hard earnings winked at by those in authority....

A race of people who, denied the right of suffrage, outraged, butchered, with their rights ruthlessly trampled upon from one end of the South to the other, would kiss the hand that smites, and beg the privilege of dying for their oppressors, is degenerate indeed, and can but merit the contempt of the people in whose cause they enlist.

Again, we voice the cry, one that we have repeatedly uttered during the past ten years: A man who is not good enough to vote for a government is not good enough to fight for it.

We do not profess to be able to keep colored men from enlisting. We are not trying to do so. We are stating the facts and they can act to suit themselves.

The flag of race prejudice has been raised. Colored companies have been barred from white regiments, and the talk is to enlist them in separate regiments and brigades.

If this be true, we insist they be commanded by colored officers.

We do not propose to be insulted and have those who insult us profit by our bravery.

In the South today exists a system of oppression as barbarous as that which is alleged to exist in Cuba, and yet those in authority at Washington could declare war, spend one hundred million of dollars, muster in one hundred and twenty-five thousand troops, and offer to spend a million dollars to feed foreigners while more than a hundred thousand people are starving in this country.

No, we do not like it, and we would be slaves indeed were we to be silent in the face of such rank injustice.

We are not a candidate for public office. Our duty is to advocate the cause of the people we represent, and about here they, with us, are saying, Mr. Editor, 'No officers; no fight!'...

The War in the Philippines

The first Spanish settlers came to the Philippine Islands in 1505 during the reign of King Philip II. They took land away from the natives and gave it to colonists, imposed forced labor, high taxes, and forbade people to practice their native religions.

During the 1890s, rebels, led by Emilio Aguinaldo, kept the country in turmoil with raids and assassinations of government officials. As tension between Spain and the United States grew, Undersecretary of the Navy Theodore Roosevelt ordered George Dewey, commander of the U. S. Pacific fleet, to leave Hong Kong and prepare to attack Manila as soon as war was declared.

On May 1, the fleet sailed into Manila Bay and started firing. The Spanish fleet was in disrepair, armed with outdated cannon, and was no match for Dewey's little fleet. Seven Spanish ships were lost and over 400 Spanish sailors died. Two American officers and nine men were slightly wounded, and the American ships received little damage.

George Dewey became a national hero. He was promoted to admiral, presented with a $10,000 Tiffany sword and a house in Washington, D. C.

This little jingle contains a clever play on Dewey's name:

Source: Deborah Bachrach, *The Spanish-American War*, San Diego: Lucent Books, 1991, p. 70.

O Dewey was the morning

Upon the first of May

And Dewey was the Admiral

Down in Manila Bay:

And Dewey were the Regent's eyes,

Them orbs of Royal Blue!

And Dewey feel discouraged?

I do not think we Dew.

(Minnesota Historical Society)

Admiral George Dewey

It seemed in their mutual interest for Aguinaldo and Dewey to use each other. Dewey promised to arm Aguinaldo's 80,000 men, of whom fewer than half had rifles. Every man had a bolo—a single blade, razor-sharp machete. Some had bows and arrows, old Spanish guns and "bamboo cannons" (iron pipes that shot broken glass and nails).

Aguinaldo believed that the Americans wanted to help free the Philippine Islands from the oppressive Spanish rule, and that the Americans would leave the islands after the Spanish were driven out. In truth, the U. S. saw the Philippines as a stepping stone to Asia.

The first contingent of American troops reached Manila in July. Most of the Americans who went to the Philippines were inexperienced, poorly-trained volunteers who wanted to go to Cuba, not to a spot on the map so insignificant that President McKinley had to look in an atlas to find out where it was. Many had no uniforms, shoes, underwear, or adequate food.

Aguinaldo agreed to let the United States take over part of the Filipino front line in the attack on Manila. The Spanish commander, General Firmin Jaudenes, fearing massacre by Aguinaldo's men, surrendered to the Americans. American troops occupied Manila, but Filipino troops were barred from entering.

On January 6, 1899, Aguinaldo broke off relations with the United States forces. The former allies prepared to fight. The Americans attacked, killing 3000 on the first day. Realizing that the Americans could not be defeated in battle, Aguinaldo began a guerrilla war that lasted until 1902. Atrocities were committed by both sides. Americans set up concentration camps and carried out policies similar to the ones Weyler had used in Cuba. General Shafter ordered the extermination of Aguinaldo's followers.

George F. Telfer, an Oregon Infantry Volunteer, was appointed Judge Advocate in Manila. His letters home clearly show the demoralization and brutality of American troops. The following excerpts are from letters written between September, 1898, and April, 1899.

Source: Sara Bunnett, *Manila Envelopes: Oregon Volunteer Lt. George F. Telfer's Spanish-American War Letters*, Oregon Historical Press, 1987, pp. 121-2, 124-5, 130-1, 153-4.

We are expecting trouble with the insurgents. Several collisions have taken place....

We still 'don't fight.' We kill a man or so every night, but that is poor satisfaction....

Stood around in the sun for several hours. Then came an order ...to go to the front. We went about two miles out and stood in the sun two hours more and watched the ambulances bringing in the wounded—a cheerful sight. The ambulance men looked like butchers, with their hands and arms covered with blood. Every now and then a gang of prisoners would be brought in....Every village or church—occupied by insurgents—was burned by our troops as soon as reached. Nothing was spared—so of course the women, children and aged people had to come into the city....

The only work our company did was Sunday...to go to a large monestery and capture 1,000 natives who had taken refuge there....

The prison is in a swampy place and the mosquitos are awful....

At 3:30 A.M. we were aroused by the cracking of rifles and zip of bullets....The next day we proceded to devastate the country. We burned every house within two miles of our camp—and drove the natives away....

At daybreak we started for Sta. Marie—an insurgent strong-hold. Aguinaldo was there with about 1,000 troops. They made slight resistance and then retreated. We burned the town and every house or rice stack near there. We marched back to the railroad leaving a trail of smoke such as this country has never seen before. We shot at every human being that came within range—paying no attention to white flags...."

On July 4, 1902, the war officially ended. Sixteen thousand Filipinos were killed, and another 200,000 died of disease, starvation and other causes. The Filipino Insurrection cost the U. S. $60 million dollars, but the higher price was the damage to America's image of nurturing the cause of freedom.

"Boots"

President William McKinley wrote an official history of the Spanish-American War. In it he gave an account of a thirteen-year-old boy who shined shoes on the streets of Pittsburgh. Nicknamed "Boots" because of his occupation, he was a stowaway when the Tenth Pennsylvania Regiment, United States Volunteers, left Pittsburgh for San Francisco. The volunteers treated him as their pet and their mascot, and he was allowed to go with them to the Philippines.

Source: Marshall Everett, editor, *Exciting Experiences in Our Wars with Spain and the Filipinos*, Chicago, Book Publishers Union, 1899, p. 189.

The ammunition of the Pennsylvanians was running short and many a brave heart was beating anxiously. Suddenly little 'Boots' scurried out of the trenches to run over a wide and exposed stretch, where the bullets flew like scud from the sea, driven over the marshes by a northeaster, and the men in the trenches forgot their own grave peril as they thought of the little lad and were not ashamed of him, but sorry in the belief that, terror-stricken, he had fled at the awful sounds of battle.

It was not long before 'Boots,' laden down with...ammunition, came staggering across the same field, facing the leaden hail, and there was a mighty cheer as he fell into the trenches with his precious burden. It was not much, but the men knew that it would mean more. The regiment was proud of its mascot and boy hero. It was not many minutes before a plentiful supply of ammunition had been given to the Pennsylvanians, and a position that was weak had been made strong and impregnable by one little bootblack.

While the fighting continued, 'Boots' was not idle. At the greatest risk of his life he hurried along the trenches distributing the needed cartridges and again he was bearing water to the wounded and the dying and to those who, exhausted in the terrific heat of the conflict, were wild for a sup of the precious water. When the battle was over 'Boots' McDermott was the hero in a regiment of heroes and the proud Pennsylvanians were loud in their praises and untiring in their efforts to do honor to a thirteen-year-old boy.

Admiral Dewey heard of the youngster and sent for him. He wanted to know that sort of a boy....The two became great friends. Dewey wisely wanted the boy to get an education that his manly courage might be used to good purpose. He sent the boy home.

Care of the Wounded

Wounded men received minimum care in primitive and unsanitary conditions, while sharpshooters harassed patients and doctors.

Source: Post, *op. cit.*, p. 135.

I ran across the man who had been shot through the belly. The purple welt was darker and a little bit of lint stuck out at each end. There was no other dressing.

'What did they do for you?' I asked.

'They took something and poked a rag in one hole and out the other,' he explained. 'Then they pulled it out and stuck in another— and pulled it back and forth. And Je-sus, did it hurt!'

Source: Creelman, *op. cit.*, pp. 212-214.

Who that was there can forget the next day, when the Spanish sharpshooters who had escaped from the village tried for hours to kill the defenceless soldiers lying in our camp? Graves were dug and the dead buried before our eyes. And although the field was strewn with torn and shattered men, no sound of complaining was heard....The rain beat upon them. The terrible tropical sun made the fever leap in their veins and dazzled their eyes. Again the rain soaked their blankets and again the sun tormented them. The bullets of skulking assassins hummed over them. Men gave last messages for their families. Men died. But not a sound of protest broke the silence. I saw more real heroism in that scene of pain than ever I saw in battle....

Vultures gathered around the camp and waited in the wet grass. Nearer they came, with hesitating, grotesque hops, watching, watching, watching. There was a horrible humor in the way they hovered....

Sergeant William Payne spoke of conditions at the field hospital.

Source: Cashin, *op. cit.*, p. 223.

The doctor set my arm and dressed it. I was then sent about two hundred yards from the hospital to sleep in the grass. I had nothing to lie on and only the sky for a cover; but I could not stay in the hospital for the sharpshooters fired on it all night.

The next morning, July 2d, being wet with my own blood and the heavy dew that fell during the night, I naturally felt miserable.

Clara Barton In Cuba

Clara Barton, the founder of the Red Cross, had served all over the world. In her seventies, she took a group of Red Cross nurses and doctors to Cuba. The following account was written by a contemporary of hers, Clara Bewick Colby, and it includes Clara Barton's own words.

Source: *Harper's Pictorial History of the War with Spain*, Harper and Brothers, NY, 1899, p. 441.

Early in the year Miss Barton had gone to Cuba and worked with the Red Cross ameliorating the suffering of the reconcentrados until the time war was declared when she returned and offered the services to the government. They were declined with the statement that the government would be abundantly able to provide for the needs of its soldiers.

Miss Barton, in the latter part of April, went South in the Texas [a U. S. ship], watching for the first opportunity which would land her in Cuba and put her in a position where she could help the reconcentrados, for whose assistance the supplies with which the Texas was loaded had been contributed. The opportunity came with the sailing of Sampson's fleet, and Miss Barton landed at Guantanamo shortly after our marines.

Reaching Siboney June 26, Dr. Lesser and others of the Red Cross officials immediately went to the hospital of the United States troops, where the wounded and dying lay on the bare floor, many without even a blanket under them, and lacking every comfort. The surgeon in charge, carrying out the policy of the surgeon-general, declined assistance. Not allowed to minister to our own soldiers, they went to General Garcia, who welcomed them and with tears of gratitude, but begged them to wait a few hours until the hospital could be made fit for them to enter. Miss Barton says graphically: 'The Red Cross nurses are not accustomed to wait when there is something that needs to be done to alleviate suffering,' and they went to work, scrubbed the floor, washed the patients and put clean night-shirts on them, and before night fell the place was a little heaven.

This hospital was just across from where our own wounded lay suffering, and some of our soldiers, going by, noticed the transformation and began to inquire how it was that the Red Cross gave them the go-by and lavished its attention on the Cubans. Their vigorous protest and the awful exigencies of that fateful period of waiting for government supplies broke through all formalities and led the army surgeons to solicit Red Cross co-operation, which was gladly given.

Stephen Crane Captures Juana Diaz

Soon after the war ended, Richard Harding Davis wrote an article about some of the war correspondents in Cuba and Puerto Rico. The following is his tribute to Stephen Crane, and the account of Crane's capturing a village single-handedly.

Source: Richard Harding Davis, "Our War Correspondents in Cuba and Puerto Rico," *Harper's New Monthly Magazine*, Vol. XCVIII, #DLXXXVIII, May, 1899, pp. 938-948.

Crane was the coolest man, whether army officer or civilian, that I saw under fire at any time during the war. He was most annoyingly cool, with the assurance of a fatalist. When the San Juan hills were taken, he came up them with James Hare, of Collier's. He was walking leisurely, and though the bullets passed continuously, he never once ducked his head. He wore a long rain-coat, and as he stood peering over the edge of the hill, with his hands in his pockets and smoking his pipe, he was as unconcerned as though he were gazing at a cinematograph.

Puerto Ricans were happy to have the Spanish forced off their island, and welcomed Americans as heroes.

At that time every town in Puerto Rico surrendered to the first American who entered it, and we thought that to accept the unconditional surrender of a large number of foreigners would be a pleasing and interesting experience....He (Stephen Crane) rode into Juana Diaz, and the town, as a matter of course, surrendered, and made him welcome. He spent the day in establishing an aristocracy among the townspeople, and in distributing largesse to the hungry. He also spent the night there, sleeping peacefully beyond our lines and with no particular interest as to where the Spaniards might happen to be. The next morning, when he was taking his coffee on the sidewalk in front of the only cafe, he was amused to see a "point" of fine soldiers advance cautiously along the Ponce road, dodging behind bushes, and reconnoitering with both daring and skill of the American invader. While still continuing to sip his coffee he observed a skirmish-line following this "point," and finally the regiment itself, marching bravely upon Juana Diaz. It had come to effect its capture. When the commanding officer arrived, his sense of humor deserted him, and he could not see how necessary and proper it was that any town should surrender to the author of the *Red Badge of Courage*.

War is Kind

Stephen Crane was already famous when he went to Cuba as a correspondent. His book, The Red Badge *of* Courage, *published in 1895, brought him fame and popularity. This powerful poem, published in 1899, contrasts the realities of war with the romantic notions that were so popular at the time.*

Source: Stephen Crane, *The Complete Poems of Stephen Crane*, ed. Katz, Joseph, Cornell University Press, Ithaca, 1972, p. 36.

Do not weep, maiden, for war is kind.
Because your lover threw wild hands toward the sky
And the affrighted steed ran on alone,
Do not weep.
War is kind.

    Hoarse, booming drums of the regiment,
    Little souls who thirst for fight,
    These men were born to drill and die.
    The unexplained glory flies above them,
    Great is the Battle-God, great, and his Kingdom—
    A field where a thousand corpses lie.

Do not weep, babe, for war is kind.
Because your father tumbled in the yellow trenches,
Raged at his breast, gulped and died,
Do not weep.
War is kind.

    Swift blazing flag of the regiment,
    Eagle with crest of red and gold,
    These men were born to drill and die.
    Point for them the virtue of slaughter,
    Make plain to them the excellence of killing
    And a field where a thousand corpses lie.

Mother whose heart hung humble as a button
On the bright splendid shroud of your son,
Do not weep.
War is kind.

Results of the War

by
Mary Alice Burke Robinson

The Treaty of Paris was signed on December 10, 1898, in which, after two years under an American military governor, Cuba was granted freedom. American troops withdrew from Cuba in 1903, but maintained a naval base at Guantanamo. Spain lost Puerto Rico and Guam, which became U. S. territories. The United States paid Spain $20 million for the Philippine Islands. Between 1899 and 1902, the United States suppressed a Filipino uprising against the new colonial power, and an era of interventionist foreign policy began for America.

In Cuba, 400 Americans died of wounds in battle. Most of the 5400 American deaths were from diseases, lack of proper treatment, and inadequate or unskilled care. Four thousand American soldiers died in the Philippine Islands.

McKinley had wisely chosen officers from both the Confederate and Union Armies to wage the Spanish-American War. This helped develop a spirit of unity in the United States, as people became more willing to put the Civil War behind them.

Britain was the only European country that sided with the United States when she went to war with Spain, and the two nations became friends. Germany had sent warships to Manila Bay after the American victory there, causing a rise in anti-German feelings.

Another result of the war was the building of the Panama Canal. This huge construction project could not have been done before Major Walter Reed, a military surgeon with the United States Army, found a successful way to combat yellow fever.

Theodore Roosevelt became a national hero. He was elected governor of New York State six weeks after his regiment disbanded on September 15, 1898. He became vice-president when William McKinley was re-elected president, and became president after McKinley's assassination on September 6, 1901.

The end of the Spanish-American War marked the emergence of the United States as a world power.

Suggested Further Reading

Note: Books cited at the beginning of each excerpt are also recommended for further reading.

Gay, Kathlyn, and Martin Gay. *Spanish-American War.* New York: Twenty-First Century Books (A Division of Henry Holt and Company), 1995.

Harper's Pictorial History of the War with Spain. New York: Harper's, 1899.

Herner, Charles H. *Cowboy Cavalry.* Tucson, Arizona: Arizona Historical Society, 1998.

Miller, Stuart C. *Benevolent Assimilation: The American Conquest of the Philippines 1899-1903.* New Haven: Yale University Press, 1982.

Milton, Joyce. *The Yellow Kids: Foreign Correspondents in the Heyday of Yellow Journalism.* New York: Harper & Row, 1989.

Musicant, Ivan. *Empire by Default: The Spanish-American War and the Dawn of the American Century.* New York: A Marian Wood Book (A Henry Holt Company), 1998.

Roosevelt, Theodore. *The Rough Riders.* Prince Frederick, Maryland: Recorded Books, Inc., 1993. (4 cassette tapes)

Tebbel, John. *The Life and Good Times of William Randolph Hearst.* New York: Dutton, 1952.

Walker, Dale L. *Bucky O'Neill: The Story of a Rough Rider.* Tucson, Arizona: University of Arizona Press, 1983.

About the Editor

Mary Alice Burke Robinson holds bachelor's and master's degrees from State University of New York, Potsdam, New York. She taught in public schools on Long Island and northern New York, and was an adjunct professor for SUNY, Potsdam, teaching graduate level courses at the Watertown, New York campus.

Mrs. Robinson and her husband, Dr. Eugene Westover Robinson, divide their time between southern Arizona and the St. Lawrence River's Thousand Islands region.

This is Mrs. Robinson's third book for Discovery Enterprises, Ltd.'s *Perspectives on History Series.* Her previous books are: *The French and Indian War: Prelude to American Independence*, and *The War of 1812.*